# MINDSET

# 21 Mindset - Improvement Tricks!

## Your Daily Guide to Achieve more Happiness, Success, Growth and Will Power in Your Life!

# Introduction

I just want to reach out to you quickly to say thank you and congratulate you for downloading the book:

**"21 Mindset - Improvement Tricks! Your Daily Guide to Achieve more Happiness, Success, Growth and Will Power in Your Life!".**

This book contains proven steps and strategies on how to Change Your Mindset and start your journey to a bright and successful future.

For you, we wanted to create a guide that is easy to read – and good to follow! If you take the chances, provided in this book and make them a habit, you can change Your Life – **Forever**!

Thanks again for downloading this book, I hope you enjoy it and it will have a wonderful impact on your life!

# Section I:
# Change Your Mindset Toward Yourself

Before you change the world around you, you must first change yourself. You can do this by following the suggestions of the upcoming six chapters. First we'll learn how to believe in yourself so that you can face your fears. Once you get out of your comfort zone and realize that you have unlimited potential, then it will be easy for you to determine your life goals.

Unfortunately, not all of our goals and dreams are achieved right away. That's why it's important to cultivate inner patience and to strive for inner peace and compassion. Once you've achieved that, then you will understand what your focus should be on in any given day. When you combine strong focus with a large dream for your life, then you can achieve everything you want. Ready to change your life? Turn the page and let's begin a journey of self-discovery.

# Chapter 1:
# **Believe In Yourself**

No matter what hardships you have faced in your life or what you were told when you were growing up, your life has meaning. You are worthy of self-love and capable of doing so much more than you've ever imagined. The first step to changing your mindset in order to find happiness, success, and growth is to start believing in yourself.

When you believe in yourself, a whole new world opens up to you. You'll interact with your surroundings and other people with a natural curiosity and wonder that comes from a growth mindset instead of limiting your possibilities through a negative fixed mindset. Here's what you can do in order to believe in yourself more, so that you can live up to your potential:

I. Return to your past. Think about all of the accomplishments that you have achieved. Ask yourself, "what have I achieved in the past year?" and "what am I happy that I've accomplished in my life?" Write down a list of your accomplishments, no matter how small your achievements are.

II. Write down the skills that you have. What skills allowed you to achieve your accomplishments? List all of the reasons why you are able to do the things that you do.

III. Write down everything that you admire about yourself. Whether it's your natural ability to connect with people, or your quiet and reserved nature. There are surely things that you enjoy about yourself which will allow you to find more opportunities to bring out your best side while interacting with others.

The simple task of writing down your past accomplishments, the things that you admire about yourself, and the skills you have is enough to boost your confidence. Whenever you're feeling low and turn your mind to a negative thought pattern, just remember everything you're good at, and all the reasons why you should be happy to be just who you are.

# Chapter 2:
# Face Your Fears

Your fears will not go away unless you face them! If you really want to expand your mind, you should be driven to do the things that scare you. There are a few things that happen when you go out on a limb and do the things that you're afraid of. First, you start to understand the misconceptions that people have about different cultures, religions, and geographical locations. Second, you expand your mind and learn that you can achieve even the things that might make your scared. Third, you expand your potential and start thinking differently because of the unique experiences that you've had.

So how do you face your fears? Here are all of the different steps you can take to turn your fears into your passions...

I. Understand that everyone has fears. Acknowledge the things that you're afraid of without feeling embarrassed or beating yourself up.

II. Write down your fears. Do you know why you are scared of these things? Make sure that whenever you overcome a fear that you wrote on this list, that you cross it off and share your new thought process on another piece of paper.

III. Are some of your fears reasonable? Some things are really scary, and rightfully so! Those really scary things that are on your list because they're really dangerous don't have to be changed. But what about your irrational fears? Determine which ones are rational and which ones are irrational, and then start changing your mindset on your irrational fears.

IV. Break down your irrational fears. Take things slowly and break down your irrational fears into smaller tasks. For instance, if you have a fear of heights, don't go to the top of the Eiffel Tower first thing! Start by going hiking to a beautiful viewpoint, taking a glass elevator to the top floor of a shopping center, or just climbing a play structure at a playground.

Once you've done all the little tasks on your list, then you can try and concur your bigger fears by sitting on a ferris wheel, going for a hot-air ballon ride, or even by skydiving! You might just find something that you're passionate about.

V. Live in the moment. While you're tackling your fears, don't worry about the future, which has not yet arrived. Focus on your breathing, relax your body, and bring yourself to the present moment.

VI. Consider your past accomplishments. That's right, you've likely done something that's even scarier or something that has led you to dispelling your fear. Just remembered how amazing it was to get over your previous fear so that you could push yourself even more at this very moment.

When you've experienced new areas of the world and discovered new passions by believing in yourself and facing your fears, then it's time to determine your life goals.

# Chapter 3:
# Determine Your Life's Purpose

What brings you happiness? What fills you with joy and passion? Think about this for a second. Perhaps you have all these things that you love, but you fail to make any progress toward achieving them because of all the other tasks that you have to accomplish each day. It's okay because you're not alone! You can start living a more fulfilling life by finding your passion by determining your life's purpose. Here's how:

I. Keep a journal. Hopefully you have already done this to list down your past accomplishments and to keep track of the fears that you've eliminated. Now it's time to take that journal and write down why you think you're on Earth, the things in life that your passionate about, and what brings you joy.

This journal is just for you, so don't try to be perfect and instead just get your thoughts out. Be 100% honest with yourself while discussing the things that you want to do with your life and it will help you determine your life path.

II. Dive deeper into your interests. Discuss the times where you have been truly happy. Write about the people who are most interesting to you. Discuss how you like to spend your time. Do you have any role models? What would you do if you only had one week to live? These prompts will help you determine the things that you are truly passionate about so that you can fill more of your time with that.

III. Discuss the people and places that you love. This will explain where your heart lies while bringing your closer to learning about the life you want to live. What would you be doing if you had no limitations? When you focus on what you love you uncover passions that go deeper than the things that you value with reason.

IV. Plan backwards. What would your ideal life be from 100 years old to now? How would you spend your time? What things would you achieve? Write down everything you want to do in order to live a life of passion. Somewhere in the process is your life passion.

After you have written about the topics listed above, then you'll be able to make goals for your life. Some of your goals you'll accomplish tomorrow. Some might only be possible in the long-term. With enough focus, dedication, and time, you'll be able to achieve the life that brings you fulfillment.

# Chapter 4:
# Allow Yourself To Be Patient

The most successful people do the work that they need to when they need to do it. But they also understand that it isn't possible to do everything. Everyone has to rely on someone else for something and not everything always goes to plan the minute that you want it to. That's why it's important to cultivate patience. Patience is what will allow you to find new opportunities, live all of your passions, and adopt a positive mindset. Here are three things to consider while building your patience:

1. Waiting makes you happier. That's right, it has been scientifically proven that if you wait for something, you value it more. Sure, it's really nice to be instantly gratified. But think about this. What are you more likely to really enjoy: a hamburger at a fast-food restaurant, or a hamburger at a full service restaurant where you have to wait? Sure the fast food might satisfy your immediate hunger needs but the enjoyment of being in a nice restaurant, the company of your friends, and a little wait for a more delicious burger will probably result in greater happiness.

2. Patience allows new opportunities to come into your life. The longer that you can wait for the perfect opportunity, the easier it will be for

you to achieve greatness when the time is right. Right now might not be the best time to invest, purchase a home, or accomplish all of your dreams. That's all right! Soon new opportunities will present themselves if you're patient, and you'll benefit from waiting until the time is right.

3. Patience changes your perception of yourself and others. It's easy to be hard on yourself or to demand that other people are perfect while in your company. The problem is that no one (yourself included) is perfect! Have patience with people and believe that they can complete what they say they will. Give them enough time to be creative, and they'll come through for you. On the same note, give yourself the time to develop fully into the person that you want to be as well.

When you live a life of patience, you're able to fully develop your skills and wait until the time is right. You see people differently and are more willing to be fluid instead of ridged. Success comes to people who are accommodating. You can find success in life if you are patient with yourself and reasonable with your expectation of others.

# Chapter 5:
# Learn How To Focus

Developing more focus will allow you to achieve more and it will also make you a happier person! When you stop focusing on the things that no longer benefit you and instead concentrate just on what will help you accomplish the goals and dreams that you have, then you'll be able to accomplish your goals. It's not always easy to reduce distractions, but if you learn how to then you'll be able to achieve more in a day then you thought possible. Here's how to increase your focus:

I. Concentrate on one thing at a time. Start by focusing on accomplishing one task for thirty minutes. In this time, don't listen to music, browse your Facebook, or check your cell phone. Just make progress toward whatever you're trying to accomplish. When the initial time has passed, continue with your task and push yourself to see how long you can keep your focus.

As time goes on, you'll build your focus. Remember, everyone needs a break of at least 7 minutes per hour of work, so when you start working for longer periods of time then make sure that you rest. Do whatever you want on your break and then come back to work promptly, again avoiding distractions. Soon you'll achieve your goals without concentrating on any of the other things that waste your time.

15

II. Meditate daily. Sit in silence in a comfortable position for a few minutes each day. Every day, push yourself to meditate for a longer period of time until you can sit for 20 minutes comfortably. Relax and focus on your breathing, while allowing any thoughts that you have to come and pass. Once you've finished, take some time to come back to your senses before getting up. This will improve your concentration and focus throughout the rest of the day if you make it a daily habit.

III. Know what you're going to do a day before you do it. That's right, keeping a to-do list is the best way to make sure that you achieve your goals. When you know what it is that you want to accomplish each day, then you will spend more time actually achieving your daily goals. Without a to-do list, you're more likely to float around from one thing to the next without actually accomplishing anything.

Once you've learned how to concentrate, determined your goals, defined your life purpose, and understand how to be patient, and then you can determine your dream. Everyone should have a vision for his or her life; so let's discuss what you can do to achieve a growth mindset.

# Chapter 6:
# Have A Dream

I consider a dream as an ultimate goal for your life. It should be something that can only be achieved over long periods of time, which bring meaning to your life and the lives of others. Some dreams might not be totally realized in your lifetime, but if you dream large enough then your dream will eventually take off and impact people around the world. Here's how you can accomplish even your wildest dreams:

I. Start with the specifics. If you're not specific about what your dream is, then you won't ever be satisfied to accomplish them. Have an idea of what you want to happen, then start working toward that, even if all of the details haven't been hashed out. As time goes on you can add more specifics to your dreams or change your dreams altogether.

II. Have the desire to accomplish your dreams. The stronger your belief in self, the more patience you've cultivated, and the easier it is for you to move out of your comfort zone, the more likely you'll be to achieve your dreams. You have to do more than just want your dreams to become a reality. If you want your dreams to transform then you have to take the appropriate steps to achieve your goals.

As you go through life, ask yourself, "does this action/thought/belief help move me closer to my dreams, or is it taking me further away from them?" Focus only on the things that help you accomplish your dreams while destroying any negative beliefs and refusing to have your time taken away from you on things that don't accomplish your goals. You have a limited amount of time to achieve what you're set out to do, so you have to manage your time well.

Take action now. There is no time like the present to begin accomplishing your dreams. Determine your goals, figure out how you're going to go from point A to point B, and then take action! Stop putting things off until tomorrow and use the time that you have right now to make a difference. Review your progress and correct yourself whenever you notice that you aren't making the best use of your time.

Everyone fails at some point. Remember to enjoy the process instead of just the outcome. This will help you focus on taking one day at a time and doing what you can with the time you have. You have to make sacrifices to accomplish your dreams, but you can remove the hurdles that block your path and achieve even the largest dream in your lifetime. All you have to do is set your mind to it, believe that you can, and take action now!

# Section II:
# Change Your Mindset Toward Others

Discussed briefly in the previous chapter, this section discusses why it's important to change your mindset when it comes to other people. Soon you'll discover how to be a better friend, family member, and business partner. If you've ever worried about relationships, you've ever lost a friend, or you want to find passion for social interactions again, then you'll love this section.

First you'll learn about the importance of surrounding yourself with good company. The people that you spend most of your time with are the ones who influence everything from your income to your level of happiness. You'll also learn about engaging with new people to increase your amount of friends. After which you'll discover why it's important to drop your judgments towards other people, how you can enjoy the experiences that you share in a group, and why it's important to help other people achieve their goals.

# Chapter 7:
# Surround Yourself With Good Company

It's vital that if you want to change your mindset toward other people, that you only surround yourself with people who are positive. If they help you grow in business, in life, or they're just fun to be around, make sure you keep them as a friend! Here are some ways that you can improve the relationships in your life and keep the people who matter to you around for the long haul:

I. Forgive for any wrongdoing. Holding on to negative energy because you didn't like the words or actions of another person only attract more negative people and situations to your life. The easier that you can forgive other people for hurting you, the easier it will be to find people who will be supportive and bring love and happiness to your life. Also remember how important it is to forgive yourself for any mistakes that you've made.

II. Be consciously aware of your thoughts. When you keep your mindset in a positive place that matches with your goals and dreams in life, then you're able to bring better people into your world. Show others the same love and respect that you want to have and you will build rewarding relationships. Everyone has different ways of communicating, different experiences, and different mindsets. Try to think about where people are coming from when something triggers you as being insensitive or inconsiderate. Chances are that they just don't hold the same values or thought patterns that you do.

# Chapter 8:
# Engage New People

Every day you have the opportunity to meet someone new. If you've ever been interested in befriending someone yet you've let the opportunity pass, now's the time to step out of your comfort zone and turn strangers into friends. Here's what you should do:

I. Put yourself out there. Yes, take a couple risks in your life! Do something that makes you scared. It's okay to speak to people that you pass on the street, and the more you get used to rejection, the easier every other encounter is to build a new relationship.

II. Understand that people are usually friendly. There's a common misconception that other people are scary. This isn't the case! The more that you open up and try to make friends with people, the easier it will be to engage new people. You'll be surprised with how easy it is to chalk up a new conversation. Hope for the best, accept things as they come, and understand that people are also living their lives. After a few interactions, you should really hit it off with someone. All it takes is a simple hello.

# Chapter 9:
# **Drop Your Judgments**

Holding judgments about other people puts you in a fixed mindset. You have to stop believing that there's only one right way to live life. People who do things differently from you aren't wrong; they're simply living differently. Everyone responds based on how they view reality. There's no reason for other people to live according to your values and when you stop placing judgment on people then you can form healthier and stronger relationships.

If you want to stop judging people, there are a few steps that you can follow. First identify that you are making a judgment about yourself, others, a place, or a situation. Next, reflect on what is occurring and why it's bringing about a negative response from you. Then determine what is possible and look past the surface of what's happening. Could it be that you don't fully realize the meaning of the person, place, or situation that you're in? Afterward, move on and continue to progress with your life instead of placing judgment. Hold positive intention and keep an open heart and mind.

# Chapter 10:
# Enjoy The Journey

People are always worried about the outcome of their actions. They of course want to achieve greatness or to accomplish something special. Sometimes it works out and sometimes it doesn't. Instead of focusing on the outcome, focus on the journey. It's the process that you take to achieve something that builds your character. The outcome is just a result of following a good process and making progress by changing yourself.

- There are a few reasons why you should focus on the process instead of the outcome which include the fact that...

- You build habits when you focus on the process. Success is achieved by forming solid habits.

- You're more confident in your ability when you focus on the process. There's work and dedication put into doing your best at all times instead of just doing something for the reward.

You're more likely to succeed if you focus on the process. If you enjoy what you're doing then you're going to do way better. If the only thing that's making you progress toward your goals is a reward, then you'll get burnt out before then.

The process will help you build patience. Rome wasn't built in a night. Your dreams won't come in one day. You have to work hard and push yourself to achieve greatness. When you set your sights on doing something to the best of your ability day after day, then you'll develop the patience to see your goals all the way through.

# Chapter 11:
# Help Someone Prosper

Sometimes it can be really difficult to put all of your projects on the sidelines so that you can help another person prosper. What you'll find however is that helping a friend, stranger, or business partner can result in some of the most successful project that you're a part of. Here are a couple ways that you can help people easily throughout your day:

I. Volunteer your time. Helping people can be as simple as volunteering once a week or a month to share an experience with your community.

II. Give people feedback. Perhaps someone has a question about a product or service that they give. Come up with constructive feedback that will assist them with their work. Although not everyone takes criticism well, if you choose your business partners correctly then your feedback can help improve their success and business efficiency.

III. Introduce people. If you know a few people that can solve someone else's problems, be the one to make the introduction. You don't have to do everything yourself, so connecting with other people who are specialists is a great way to achieve more with relationships.

# Section III:
# Become a better You!

Life is all about improving ourselves. Become the best 'Version of Yourself' possible can be described as the ultimate goal of this journey.

With the tips and strategies in the next chapters I want to help you to make the next step. Dive into the power that lies deep within yourself and sharpen your mindset to release this power for the best possible impact on your future.

# Chapter 12:
# Know Your Purpose and Find A Vision

Why are you where you are in life right now? Why are you waking up every morning and is it to do something that you love? Even if you have a six figure a year salary, a huge home, a couple cars, and the lifestyle that you want, that doesn't mean that you're a happy person. Unless you're doing what you love to do, you'll never consider yourself a success, even with material belongings. That's why it's so important to have a life purpose.

Finding your life purpose is easy. Take out a sheet of paper and write down all of the reasons why you do the things you do. Ask yourself, "what's my true purpose in life." Once you've come up with an answer that makes you emotional, then you've found the solution.

Once you've found your purpose, you have to locate your vision. What's guiding you through your actions for the next few months? How do you know when you're going down the right path to achieve your life purpose? The answer should be in your vision. Take a little time to write out how you'll get to where you want to go. Define how you will achieve your life purpose and edit it whenever you need. This will help motivate you to achieve success when things get rough.

# Chapter 13:
# Challenge Yourself By Taking Risks

It's really easy to avoid doing the things that we want in life because of the risk that's involved in being happy. That's right... you'd rather be miserable in life with a career that you don't like than do what makes you happy. Why you ask? Because it's so comfortable to conform to the status quo. There's a solution to this however. It's called taking a risk.

First off, if you've considered taking a risk and have decided against it then you're not alone. Most people focus only on what can go wrong and limit themselves before ever getting close to success. The funny thing is that people usually overestimate the probability that something will go wrong while ignoring the potential benefits by magnifying our imaginations.

So instead of acting, most people just stick to the normal everyday activities. But think about this, what are you giving up by being inactive? Things aren't going to dramatically change in your life unless you do. When you play it safe, you stay at the same point that you've always been in while the issues in your life grow larger.

So how do you learn how to take risks?

- Plan out your method of action.

- Have faith that you'll succeed.

- Execute your plan.

- Evaluate your performance.

- Think about the next goal and repeat.

It's simple isn't it? Start looking at the positives and weighing it just as much as the negatives, and you'll begin to find the benefit in going after your goals and dreams instead of waiting for them to come to you.

# Chapter 14:
# Be Discerning

There is so much information flying at you daily, especially with modern technology such as smart phones, televisions, and computers. When you're able to ignore all of the fluff information so that you can focus on what's truly important, then you've learned how to be discerning.

Choose what you focus your energy on. Actively decide how you will or will not spend your time. Don't be afraid to let other people do the work that you don't have the time or the passion to do. Then reflect on how you've been spending your time and determine whether it's helping you achieve your goals and dreams, or whether it's stopping you from doing something more productive.

You have limited time and endless options on how to spend it. At some time you'll have to learn to say no. You need to organize and protect your time from people and things that don't require it. You also have to maximize your time doing the things that you actually love doing. It might be difficult to do at first, but with enough self-reflection it's totally possible.

# Chapter 15:
# Learn From Your Failures

If you want to succeed in anything you do, then you have to learn from your failures and use what you've learned to progress forward. It's this simple - GET OVER IT! Nearly half of businesses fail within three years. But the only entrepreneurs that really fail are the ones who don't get back up and try again. Everyone else learns from their failings and uses it to find a successful business model.

If you're ready to succeed then you should follow these simple tips:

I. Understand what it takes to be successful at whatever you want to accomplish before beginning.

II. Determine your strengths and weaknesses. Get an outside perspective and have them tell you whether you're as competent as you think you are in your chosen field.

III. Continue to build your strengths if you aren't yet ready for the responsibility of your dreams or goals if you need to. Or bring in other people to assist you with their expertise so that you can accomplish your goal together.

IV. Plan ahead to be successful. Know what your expectations are for the month. What do you want to achieve? How did your previous month differ? Then use that information to make a plan to succeed.

# Chapter 16:
# Try Something New

In order to really achieve a success mindset, you have to continually progress toward your goals. When you feel like you are growing then you find the necessary fuel that's needed to continue your work. Unfortunately there are often roadblocks, which hinder people from achieving the success that they desire. Negative mindsets, fear of the unknown, and fear of growth are just a few of them. If you want to reduce your negative mindset and allow a growth mindset to take over, then you need to move out of your comfort zone.

Sometimes all you need to do to bust out of your comfort zone is to have a new experience. This can include:

- Trying new foods.

- Changing your daily routine.

- Taking a course or class.

- Saying hello to people.

- Learning a new skill or hobby.

- Reading a book that you normally wouldn't read.

You don't have to step out of your comfort zone alone. You have other people that can attend an event with you. Sometimes this makes things easier. The important step is to not be intimidated by new settings if you want to be successful, and to instead focus on doing something that expands your horizons.

# Section IV:
# Change Your Money Mindset

Everyone has a different relationship with money. If you feel like money is a scarce commodity that there's never enough of, it seems that you need to change your mindset toward money. Money is a means to accomplish your dreams and should never be your sole reason for doing something. This section discusses how you can go about repairing your connection with money so that you can use it to fuel your passions.

First you'll learn about the importance of doing what you love. When you follow your heart, the money will also follow. Sometimes it's a sacrifice to do what you love instead of what brings the most income, which is why immediately after you'll learn the reasons why you should be grateful for the things that you have. Once you're grateful for the money that you've already earned, then you can learn how to budget, save, and invest so that you can fund your future lifestyle, goals, and dreams.

# Chapter 17:
# Do What You Love

Why is it important to do what you love? Doing what you love has been proven to increase your salary. That's because if you do what you enjoy what you do then you're happier in the workplace, you're more competent, and you do the work with more focus. Doing what you love isn't a dream either! Here are some ways that you can turn what you love to do into your career:

Do it on the side. Starting your own part-time home based business is one of the best ways to legally reduce your tax liability, meet people who are interest in the same things you do, and have a good time working in the way that you want to work. If you're not ready to switch careers just yet, consider starting your own business until you've earned enough income to let it take off.

Keep learning and improving. The more that you learn about your passion, the more likely you'll be able to turn it into something that earns you an income. If you enjoy staying at home and raising children, perhaps you can turn that into a daycare center job and get paid to watch kids. Maybe you like baseball a lot. Have you thought about hosting a podcast or writing a blog to discuss your passion?

The opportunities with current technology are endless. If you want to make the switch from a job that you hate to doing what you love to do then:

I. Determine what you're passionate about.

II. Learn how you can earn an income from what you love to do.

III. Do it part time until it takes off.

IV. And make it your primary source of income when you have the chance.

# Chapter 18:
# Be Grateful For What You Have

Being grateful for what you has doesn't just make you aware of how blessed you are in life. It also gives you an appreciation for your hard work and the work of others, and leads to a happier and healthier life. Here's how you can adopt a more grateful attitude to bring about a positive mindset:

I. Write down everything that you are grateful for each day. You still have your journal from section I right? If so, start listing down the things that you are happy for each day. If you're ever down, reflect on these things and find happiness in what you have.

II. Be mindful. There are so many things to be excited about each day. With a little mindfulness you can cultivate inner happiness as well. All you have to do is start acknowledging everything that you have and everything you receive on a daily basis.

III. Share your appreciation with someone else. If someone is meaningful in your life, let him or her know that you care. It's easy to overlook the importance of other people in our lives and it's important that we share how we feel in the time that we're given.

IV. Say thank you. Sometimes that's all you need to do.

With these tips you'll be grateful for what you have. This allows you to change your mindset to a growth mindset so that you can allow money and positivity to flow into your life.

# Chapter 19:
# Budget Carefully

What you do with your money is important if you want to use it to fuel your passions and dreams. Establishing a budget will change how you feel about money and teach you that it is possible to save and invest money for the future. Here are some tips for budgeting your hard earned money:

I. Start by tracking your income. Learn the different alternatives you have to spend your money toward and choose the options that meet your needs and your budget.

II. Make a budget and try your best to stick to it.

III. When you blow your budget in one category, don't give up and stop budgeting. If you learn from your mistakes then you can catch up the next month and continue on your plan for success.

IV. Make your budget realistic. Give yourself enough margin to allow for any unexpected expenses. That way, you still have money to save at the end of the month.

# Chapter 20:
# Learn How To Save

When you budget, the goal should be to save and invest your money. If you want to save more, you can follow these simple tips:

I. Set small goals. You don't have to save all your income at once. Small amounts of savings add up in the long run. Start small and work your way up when you can.

II. Minimize your expenses. If you have to move to have money to save each month then do so. Pay off your debts. This will allow you to save more money each month since it won't be tied up in debt payments.

III. Pay yourself first. Look at your savings as your most important expense. What you save can help you earn an income in the future without working. It can also be used to fuel your future goals and dreams.

IV. Cut back in certain categories. How much of your spending isn't moving you toward achieving your goals? Perhaps there are some areas that you can reduce or remove altogether so that you can fund your goals instead. Make the necessary sacrifices that you need to in order to fund your dreams.

# Chapter 21:
# Invest Your Earnings

When you have built up your savings then it's time to start investing. Of course, leave some for an emergency fund. If you hold the belief that investing is difficult, then it's time for you to get out of your fixed mindset! It's very simple to do with mutual funds, which over 40% of American households invest in. You simply choose a group of companies that you'd like to invest in and BOOM, you have a diversified portfolio of stocks. Here's how you can go about investing from the comfort of your own home.

I. Save up $500 to $1,000.

II. Look up online brokerage accounts. Make sure to educate yourself on the pros and cons of each one and determine which account your want to open.

III. Apply to the brokerage account online and wait to be approved.

IV. Fund your account and select how you'd like it to be invested.

As you see, investing can be made simple. Always ask for advice from a trusted advisor beforehand, as they might have some additional tips for you. Once you've learned how to save and invest then your mindset toward money should change rapidly!

# Conclusion

I hope this book was able to help you to discover how you can change your limiting beliefs, adopt a positive mindset, and accomplish more in your life than you ever thought possible. YOU CAN CHANGE! Start to Shape Your Future!

The next step is to make your actions match your mindset! You can achieve all of the things that you want if you put enough conscious effort into your goals.

Write down the essence of what you learned and what you want to integrate in your  - All Day Life! I attached a checklist down below – so you can start – NOW!

# A few words from the Author:
# E.N. Richardson

*Dear Reader of this book. Thank You! For your support and trust – buying this book! I really hope that I was able to help you. Stay on your path of Self-Improvement. I experienced myself what a great impact this can have on your future. I once read a quote from someone that I carry with me and that I want to share with you:*

**'If you are willing to do the work – You can Have Anything!'_ unknown author**

*You bought this book – this shows that you are willing to do the work. You are ahead of so many other people because, most people only want to improve and succeed, but are not willing to do whatever it takes to achieve it! Keep working on yourself!*

*If you need more valuable tips to improve yourself take a look at my other books down below! Or visit my authors page on Amazon here: E. N. Richardson*
*All the best for you!*

*I highly appreciate your support by leaving a **Review on Amazon here**.*
*This really helps!*

*Yours"*

**E. N. Richardson**

## Note from the publisher: be-to-ce publishing

If you have any questions ideas or tips around this book or the general work of E.N. Richardson feel free to connect with us at any time:

Contact:
http://be-to-ce.com

# Other books from bestselling Author E. N. Richardson:

**\*Reference Guide to Communication\***
**How to Win Friends and Master to Lead Conversations.**
**Effective and Easy Small Talk & Crucial Conversation Tactics!**

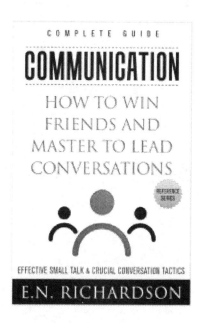

## What you will find inside the book:

- Rock-solid advice that carried thousands of people up the

ladder of success in their business- and personal lifes

- How to make people like you instantly
- How to win people to think your way
- How to never run out of words again
- How to change people's behavior – the smart way

# EMOTIONAL INTELLIGENCE (EQ)
## 7 effective Methods & EQ Secrets!
## Leverage Your Success & Happiness!

## Simple Life Changer!

- Release Your Power of Emotional Intelligence
- Understand Yourself and Others Better
- Improve Your Success in Managing Your Relationships
- proven for Business and Private
- 7 effective methods to Master your Emotional Intelligence

## 21 Self-Help Methods
## Overcome Anxiety, Fear and Depression
## Boost Happiness, Confidence & Success!

Author: *"I Want To Help You - To Help Yourself! PERIOD*

This was the simple goal - creating this book for YOU! It was a pleasure creating this book and I hope that the self-help techniques discussed here help you on your journey through a passionate and exciting life."

**Section I: Limiting The Negatives**
Overcoming Anxiety / Defeating Fear
Coping With Depression / Outdoing Anger
**Section II: Increasing The Positive**

Allowing Happiness In Your Life
Creating Confidence / Being Moved By
Motivation

57835541R00034

Made in the USA
Lexington, KY
25 November 2016